Log Cabin in the W[...]

A True Story about a Pioneer Boy

Joanne Landers Henry

Illustrated by
Joyce Audy Zarins

SCHOLASTIC INC.
New York Toronto London Auckland Sydney

TO ANNE JOHNSTON ROSS

The author wishes to thank . . . Ruth Fark Banta, who suggested that
Oliver Johnson's story be published as a children's book; Dennis
Kovener, research librarian/archivist, Conner Prairie, an outdoor his-
tory museum in Indianapolis, Indiana, for contributing to the research;
Carolyn Hessong Hickman and Robert Hessong, Ph.D., grand-
children of Howard Johnson, for permission to use material from
A Home in the Woods by Howard Johnson (published by the Indiana
Historical Society, 1951, and Indiana University Press, 1978); and
the librarians of the Indiana Historical Society, the Indianapolis–
Marion County Public Library, and the Indiana State Library,
Indianapolis, for their expert assistance.

Text copyright © 1988 by Joanne Landers Henry.
Illustrations copyright © 1988 by Joyce Audy Zarins.
The text of this book is set in 14 point Garamond No. 3.
The illustrations are drawn in pen-and-ink.
All rights reserved. Published by Scholastic Inc., 730 Broadway, New York, NY 10003, by
arrangement with Macmillan Publishing Company.
Printed in the U.S.A.
ISBN 0-590-46591-0

2 3 4 5 6 7 8 9 10   34   99 98 97 96 95 94 93

CONTENTS

....

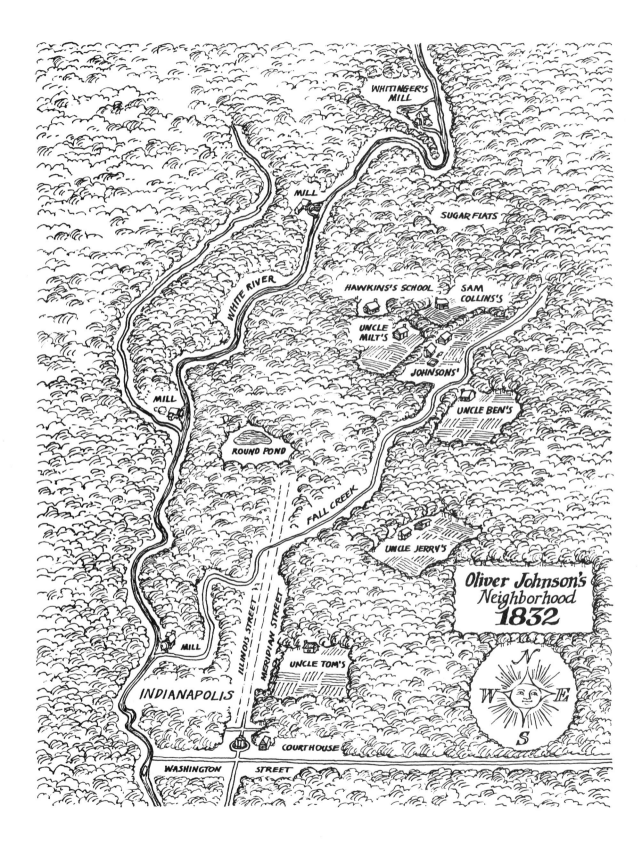

....

ONE

January

On a clear, frosty January morning in 1832, wisps of smoke rose from the chimney of a small log cabin deep in the Indiana woods. Snowflakes sparkled in the sunlight as they drifted downward from the branches of giant trees. The trees crowded close to the rear of the cabin, giving it shelter from winter storms and shade from the hot summer sun.

Inside the cabin eleven-year-old Oliver Johnson shook the snow off the bedcovers that he shared with his younger brother Luther. During the night icy flakes had sifted in through a crack in the wooden roof. Luther yanked the blanket over his head. Under another blanket nearby were two small lumps, their brothers Volney and Newton, aged five and two. But they did not stir.

Ollie paid no attention to the crisp cold of the loft. He grabbed his shirt and britches and scampered down the ladder to the floor of the cabin's one room.

Baby Elizabeth woke with a cry. Mother and Pap were just beginning to stir. Ollie's other sisters, Louisa and Lucinda, seemed to be still asleep in the bed they shared, which was in the corner of the room opposite their parents'.

Hurriedly Ollie dressed by the warmth of the glowing log coals in the huge fireplace. The smell of smoke tickled his nose, and the cold made his bare feet ache. But he liked to be the first one up, just to prove he was not a lazybones. Besides, Pap was not one to tolerate slowness when there were chores to be done.

Quietly he opened the cabin door. The farm's wide clearing in the woods was spread out before him. Sugar maples, walnut trees, and a few ash trees and oaks made a living wall around the clearing's edge. Wild grapevines twisted round some of them and clung to their branches, ends dangling down to the ground. Ollie had heard tell that this forest was one of the most beautiful in the whole world. He had no reason to doubt it.

He ran through the thin dusting of snow, one of the few snowfalls he had seen this winter. Pap's hound dog, Champ, met him at the barn, tail wagging. The barn was just large enough to shelter the horses, Nell and Jack; a cow; Pap's team of oxen, Buck and Bright; a few chickens; and the two-wheeled oxcart. The hogs just ran wild in the woods. Pap didn't pen them up until he wanted to fatten them for eating.

Ollie fed the oxen hay and water before he took care of the other animals. Pap was mighty particular about Buck and Bright. He could go places with them that he couldn't with a horse. The snapping and cracking of twigs underfoot in the woods, branches and bushes scraping the horses' legs and ribs, and the sudden

2

sounds of small animals running through the leaves would startle Nell or Jack. But Buck or Bright would just blink their eyes, slow like, and keep on going, as if nothing had happened.

"One good thing," Ollie said to himself. "I don't have to fetch the firewood anymore." This would be Luther's chore now that he was seven.

"Look see," Ollie called to Champ when his chores were finished. He stood in the barn doorway and squinted against the brightness of the sunlight on the snow as he looked out over the clearing. "Ain't that a sight!" Rough rail fences made of split logs outlined the fields. Stacked ten rails high, the fences snaked and zigzagged their way over the land. Worm fences, Pap called them. In most of the fields bent and broken cornstalks made an untidy pattern of stubble. Tree stumps dotted the open spaces farthest from the barn, with several patches of dead trees near them where Pap planned to clear the land for more fields.

Giving Champ a pat on the head, Ollie headed back toward the cabin. As he opened the door he could smell the johnny-cake—Mother's good corn bread—baking at the fireplace and the spicewood tea brewing in a pot hung over the fire.

"Don't you let that dog sneak inside, Ollie," Mother warned.

Ollie was quick to do as he was told. Because Mother had started breakfast, all the children and Pap, too, had scattered away from the fireplace. This was where Mother did all the cooking for the family, and she wouldn't tolerate any foolishness when she was working. She was a little woman, but Pap and Ollie and the others knew from experience that her temper caught fire easily. Pap said that showed she had a lot of spunk. Spunk, Ollie knew, was wood that caught fire right quick.

After bringing in a second load of wood, Luther scrambled up to the loft to get his younger brothers out of bed. Baby Eliza-

3

beth's crying could be heard over the boys' noisy shouts and thumpings from above. Louisa, who was two years older than Ollie, tried to quiet the baby, with three-year-old Lucinda's help.

Suddenly Pap stomped his foot on the floor. "That's enough rumpus up there, boys." The sounds from above stopped right away. Pap wasn't one to tolerate a lot of noise from children. Then Pap turned to Ollie. "I'm of a mind to send you to the gristmill today. You know the way."

"But, Pap . . ." Ollie began. Though he had gone with Pap many times, he had never made the trip to the mill by himself. He was afraid something might go wrong.

"A family like ours can't last long without good fresh cornmeal, Ollie," Mother put in. "We're lucky the creeks haven't froze over yet this winter, so the mill is still grinding." At the gristmill, which used water power to turn the large millstones, the miller would grind the Johnsons' shelled corn into cornmeal.

4

This was used to make the settlers' main dishes. Mother was mighty particular about having a good store of it, and she fussed if her supply of it wasn't fresh. This meant that a trip to the mill had to be made every two or three weeks.

Ollie knew it was no use telling Mother or Pap he was afraid. Pap had made up his mind, and that was that. But Ollie's fears kept coming. What if a bear got him? he wondered. Or what if he spilled the corn accidentally while he was riding through the woods? It was a long trip to make all by himself.

What Pap called his neighborhood stretched for miles. The Whitinger Mill lay three miles to the north, on the wide, winding White River. A few minutes' walk to the east of the cabin was a shallow, wide ribbon of water called Fall Creek. South about four miles was the village of Indianapolis, capital of the state. And about a quarter of a mile to the south of the cabin was a well-worn east–west trace, or track, wide enough for an oxcart to roll along. This led west to White River. But there was a lot of unknown forest in between the places Ollie knew about.

The more Ollie thought about the trip to the mill, the more poorly he felt. It would take most of the day to get there, wait for the corn to be ground, and then make the trip back home.

After breakfast was over, Pap went out to the barn to load Nell with the homemade linen bag filled with corn. As soon as the cabin door shut behind Pap, Ollie felt certain he was getting a stomachache. "Mother, my stomach is feeling poorly," he said.

She looked him in the eyes. "You do look a mite off-color, and that's a fact," she said, shaking her head. "I expect you've got a touch of mill pains. I'll have a nice helping of persimmon pudding waiting for you when you get back home. Maybe by then you'll feel good enough to eat it." And with that she sent him out to the barn.

Ollie had some trouble managing his mill pains as he rode

along the trail. One worry after another crowded into his imagi-
nation. To add to his troubles, a mass of fallen leaves covered the
trail, soggy from the fall rain and winter snow. Slippery footing
for a horse, Ollie knew.

Every now and then Nell snorted and shied when a low
branch brushed against her ribs. And her ears pricked up and
twitched every time she heard a twig snap or a rustling sound in
the leaves covering the forest floor.

Ollie recalled that wolves and a panther had been seen over
at Round Pond not long ago, and this thought frightened him.
He took a good look at the forest around him. High overhead the
sunlight glittering through the tree branches made the forest
seem peaceful and friendly enough. After all, he thought, Round
Pond was well to the south and west of his trail. He should be
safe enough here.

Suddenly Nell's right front foot slipped. "Steady, Nell,
steady!" Ollie cried. He grabbed hold of the bag of corn and
hung on tight. Nell bumped into a dead branch but caught herself before she fell. The bag saved her from being poked in the
ribs, but the branch made a hole in the bag.

"Easy, Nell." Ollie soothed her with quiet talk, though his
heart was thumping with fright. Then he saw a small, steady
stream of corn spilling from the bag. "Oh, no!" he cried.

He jerked his hat from his head and stuffed a corner of it in the hole. But he had already lost about as much corn as Mr. Whitinger, the miller, would need for his toll, or payment. Pap, like the other settlers, didn't have money. He paid his debts by trading something he had for something he needed. He couldn't afford to lose any corn.

Ollie knew he would be in serious trouble when he told Pap. Every kernel of corn counted when there was a big family to feed. Gently he coaxed Nell along, careful not to lose any more corn. By now it wasn't much farther to the mill.

When Mr. Whitinger saw the tear in the bag, he asked Ollie about it. Ollie told the miller what had happened. "Nell slipped—I couldn't stop her," he said in a worried tone.

Mr. Whitinger smiled. "Now, don't you fret, boy. I'll mend your sack while the corn is grinding. You tell your pap what happened, and I won't take any toll. John Johnson is a good man, and I've a notion that you take after him. You plugged that hole up right fast. Your quick thinking saved most of the corn."

Ollie let out a sigh of relief. He felt proud, too, about what Mr. Whitinger said about him being like Pap. "I'm mighty grateful, Mr. Whitinger," he finally managed.

That evening, after he got safely back to the cabin with the freshly ground cornmeal, he discovered Mother was right. The mill pains had gone. And the persimmon pudding tasted better than any he'd ever had.

February

There was more wet, heavy snow covering the cabin, clearing, and barn than Ollie had ever seen. It was so heavy, it bent the branches of the trees and dropped onto the forest floor.

"I'm not easy in my mind about sending Ollie and Louisa through the woods to school today, John," Mother fussed to Pap. "The trail is all snowed over, and it's still snowing. They'll get lost for sure."

"No need to fret so, Sarah," Pap answered easily. "The snow is bound to stop soon."

Some pioneer children got little or no schooling. Not many settlers bothered about book learning. But Mother and Pap set great store by reading, writing, and arithmetic. To them education was important, and they believed in a full day of learning. School opened early in the morning, when the schoolmaster called, "Come to books!"

The school Ollie and Louisa went to was about a mile and a half northwest of their cabin. Last year they had gone to a one-room school closer to home, but during the summer it had burned down. Some said an unhappy scholar set fire to it, but no one knew for sure.

This year they went to Master Hawkins's school, which was held in his cabin. He was a big man, jolly and good-natured, so Ollie didn't fret too much about being exposed to learning. There were about fifteen children of all ages. The oldest scholar was seventeen-year-old Jed Fuller. Most folks took him to be full grown and too old to go to school. But he said he liked learning better than farming, so every year he went back to school. He bragged to the younger scholars that he might go to Indiana College at Bloomington someday. It was located about fifty miles south of Indianapolis.

There wasn't any road or even a well-worn path through the dense forest to Master Hawkins's. So when school began for the year Pap had blazed a trail for the children to follow. He had marked the trail by cutting notches in the bark of the trees along the way. Ollie had felt he was being treated like a baby, but he had known better than to sass Mother or Pap.

Yet as he and Louisa left the cozy cabin behind, Ollie was glad for the blaze marks. He had never seen the forest look the way it did this morning. The heavy, wet blanket of snow changed bushes into white mounds and shrank fences until they seemed only a few rails high. Tree stumps disappeared from sight in the field where the oats had grown.

As the children traveled farther and farther away from the cabin, only the ax marks on the tree trunks looked familiar.

"Ollie, are you sure we're going the right way?" Louisa asked. "Everything looks so different."

"'Course," Ollie answered. "Can't you see Pap's marks?" But

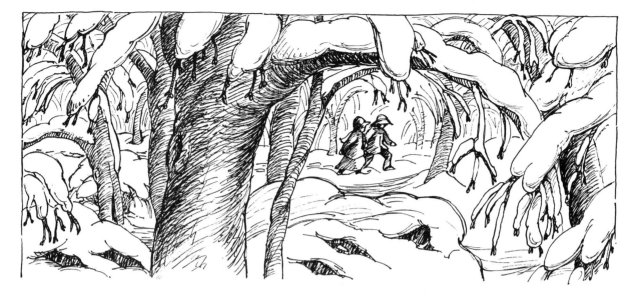

he had to admit he wasn't as sure of himself as he let on.

Ollie and Louisa were deep into the woods when they lost sight of the blaze marks on the trees. One minute the marks were there. The next minute they were gone. The two tried to retrace their steps and find the trail again. But the more they searched, the more mixed up they became. The deep snow had changed their familiar forest into a strange place, filled with unfamiliar outlines and shapes.

Ollie stopped at last and turned to Louisa, who was following in his footsteps. "We're lost, Louisa, and that's a fact!"

"Oh, Ollie!" Louisa wailed. "I'm scared. What can we do?"

Ollie thought for a minute. Then suddenly he said, "I know! We'll head north through the trees." Jed Fuller, he knew, lived to the east of the school. "If we can find Jed's tracks, all we have to do is turn left and follow them straight to school. We're almost sure to pick up his tracks," he added, "now that it's stopped snowing."

Ollie thought north was one direction, and Louisa thought it was another. But at last they agreed on a direction and set off to see if they could find the tracks.

They had gone only a short way when Ollie spotted some marks in the snow. They led off to his left.

"Maybe these tracks are Jed's," he remarked. "But they don't show very plain," he added, puzzled.

"Maybe they're not Jed Fuller's," Louisa said fearfully. "Maybe they belong to a panther or a wolf."

Ollie had to admit he didn't know for sure that they were Jed's. But following them was better than doing nothing, he felt. After all, they might lead somewhere.

After a short distance the prints turned sharply to the right, around a fallen tree. But instead of straightening out on the other side, they began to twist and turn through the woods, winding around trees and bushes.

"Looks like Jed is as lost as we are," Ollie said, still puzzled.

Tears began to trickle down Louisa's cheeks. Ollie was scared, too, but he didn't aim to let Louisa know this. Winding and twisting through the trees, the prints led them on and on.

"Ollie, look!" Louisa cried. He looked up and saw that they were at the edge of a clearing. There, on the opposite side, was a cabin nestled in the snow. Smoke curled lazily from its chimney. It was a mighty welcome, friendly sight, Ollie thought. It meant someone was most likely inside.

Without stopping to think whose cabin it might be, Ollie ran to the door and pounded on it. Louisa ran close behind him. Suddenly the door opened, and there stood Aunt Polly and Uncle Milt.

"Land sakes!" Aunt Polly cried. "I never thought to see you two today."

Ollie and Louisa were so surprised, they didn't know what to say. They weren't far from home after all! For Aunt Polly and Uncle Milt's cabin was on Pap's land.

As soon as the surprise wore off, Ollie and Louisa told their aunt and uncle how they got lost, and how scared they had been, and how they had found their way to the cabin.

Uncle Milt slapped his knee and gave a hoot of laughter. "You young ones was most likely following the tracks of your Aunt Polly's cow, Tilly. She just wandered back to the barn a little while ago. She must have been out browsing in the woods again."

Aunt Polly didn't laugh. She hugged Ollie and Louisa, then said, "I've got just what you two need." Then she gave them some warm milk to drink.

At last the sky cleared, taking away the threat of more snow. At noon Aunt Polly sent them on their way home. "No sense going on to school with half the day gone," she said.

Mother was happy to see them home safe, and Pap couldn't help laughing when he heard about Aunt Polly's cow.

THREE

March

S ome folks," Mother liked to say, "are too lazy to clear the twigs off their fireplace hearth." But Pap went at clearing trees off his land as if it were no work at all. Ollie, too, liked to work in the woods more than anything else. There was always a chance that he might find a "Look-see!"—something new to look at and wonder about.

Each year Pap added two or three acres to his farm. He said the more mouths he had to feed, the more land he needed. To him and the other settlers, children weren't much account until they were of a size to do some work.

When the sap began to rise in the sugar-maple trees, Pap stopped work in the clearing so he could go into the woods and make maple sugar. The forested land that stretched between the cabin and White River to the north was known as the Sugar Flats. Many fine sugar maples grew here. Some were four feet thick, and the tallest were almost eighty feet high.

Their bark still showed the scars where the Indians had tapped them for sap. The Indians had left these parts now, but the sugar maples were still growing. Now Pap tapped them, same as the Indians had.

He cut a **V**-shaped notch about three inches into each tree and then put a small spout in it. The sap trickled down the spout and dripped into a small trough on the ground. Each trough held about a gallon, Pap reckoned. When the troughs were full, it was time to collect the sap.

"You boys help me gather the sap," Pap said to Ollie and Luther, handing each of them a bucket. Volney and Newton wanted to help too. Pap said their place was with the womenfolk until they were of a size to work. But he let them come along for a while when they promised to stay out of his way.

After Pap and the boys poured the sap into a big kettle, he built a fire under it right there in an open space in the woods. He was careful to keep the fire steady, at just the right temperature. Slowly the sap boiled down—sugar water, Pap called it—until at last it began to turn to syrup. Pap then drained the thick syrup off from the sap; more boiling made the syrup turn to sugar. This and honey were the only sweeteners settler families like his had, so he was very particular about the making of it.

"Mind the fire—don't get too close," Pap warned the children. "Louisa, you keep a close eye on the young ones."

"Yes, Pap," Louisa answered.

"I'll watch out for them too," Ollie offered, paying little attention to Louisa. He knew what Pap was worried about. He recalled that a neighbor girl had been badly burned last summer. Her long skirt had brushed against a glowing log when she got too close to the cook fire outside her family's cabin. Pap said it was carelessness that caused the trouble. Mother said that what happened should be a lesson to them all.

When Pap returned to the job of clearing land in March, the school term was ended and Ollie was able to work all day.

"You're of a size to handle a broadax now, Ollie," Pap said. "So you come along and trim the branches off the felled trees."

"Can I come too, Pap?" Luther begged. He wasn't one to move very fast when it came to working, Ollie knew, but he didn't want to be left behind.

Pap nodded his head as he left the cabin. Mother called to Luther as he ran after Pap.

"You stay clear of where your pap fells those trees, Luther," she warned him. Every once in a while she heard tell of a child getting hurt or killed by a falling tree. "Just plain carelessness," Pap remarked. But still Mother worried.

At the far end of the clearing was a large patch of dead trees. "This is called a deadening—on account of the trees are dead," Pap explained to Luther as they drew near the patch. "I killed these trees three years ago." Pap showed the boys how he had cut through the bark and partway into the sapwood of each tree with his broadax. The cut girdled the tree trunk, which meant it ran all the way around it. This kept the sap from going up to the leaves. Without the sap the leaves died. Then, without the leaves, the tree died. Dead wood was much easier to cut than the green wood of a living tree. And because the wood was dry, it burned well.

Right next to this deadening, Pap had two other deadenings. One he had made two years ago, and one he had made last year. This made it possible for him to clear land for new fields every year. Some settlers claimed that deadenings made in the dark of the moon during June, July, and August were the best. Ollie didn't know in his own mind how true this was. But last year he saw the leaves of certain trees begin to wilt just a few hours after their trunks had been girdled during that time of the moon in June.

From where Ollie was working on a tree that had been felled earlier, he could faintly hear the *thwack-thwack* of Pap's ax. Ollie was a safe distance away, but Luther had disappeared from sight. Ollie remembered that the last place he had seen Luther was by the brush pile at the edge of the woods. Suddenly there was a loud crack, like a rifle shot. Dead-wood branches popped and snapped as a large tree began to fall. Crashing down, it broke off several smaller trees in its path.

That was what Pap had wanted it to do, Ollie knew. Felling trees was dangerous work. But Pap was a good timber man. He could throw a tree so that it dropped just where he wanted.

"Luther!" Ollie called. That's just like Luther—disappearing faster than a rabbit down a hole when there's work to be done, he thought. "Luther!" he called again. There was still no answer. Angry, he hurried deeper into the woods to search for his younger brother.

"Most likely he's up a tree playing possum—pretending he's dead. He'll just sit there real quiet like those little animals do so he can give me a scare," Ollie said to himself. "Wait till I catch him!" He shook his head.

Then he heard Champ barking. The sound came from near the edge of the woods. He ran toward it. There was Champ, tail wagging, standing next to something on the ground. As Ollie

came closer he saw that it was Luther. His left arm was twisted beneath his body, and his eyes were closed.

"Luther, you get up from there. I ain't got no time to fuss with you playing possum. I've got work to do." But Luther didn't move. Ollie was puzzled. Luther couldn't have been hit by the falling tree; he was nowhere near where it lay. He was about to give Luther a shake when he saw that his brother's arm was bloody. He must have hurt it, then fainted or been knocked out, Ollie thought. He knew he should fetch Pap, to get Luther home as soon as possible. Mother would know what to do. She was good at doctoring.

Ollie ran and fetched Pap as fast as he could. Pap carried Luther home without saying a word. As Pap laid him on the bed Luther opened his eyes. His sisters and little brothers crowded around, curious.

"Your arm is broken, Luther," Mother explained after taking a look at it. Pap asked Luther how he got himself in such a fix.

Sniffling and with tears running down his cheeks, Luther told Pap that he fell out of a tree.

"You and I will have a talk later. Right now we had best put some splints on that arm so it will heal right proper." He sent Ollie out to bring in a few pieces of yellow poplar. It was a soft wood and easy to cut or whittle. "You'll find some down on the woodpile, Ollie," he said.

While Pap waited for Ollie to return, Mother brewed a cup of peppermint-leaf tea for Luther. "You do land in a barrel of trouble sometimes, Luther," she scolded. "But the tea will make you feel better," she added more gently as she handed Luther a tin cup filled with the steaming hot liquid.

Luther was trying not to cry anymore, though his arm hurt a lot. He sat up and drank the tea.

Soon Ollie returned with the pieces of poplar. Right away he and Pap whittled some thin splints from them. Then Mother bound them onto Luther's arm with strips of clean linen.

Ollie could see she knew just how to care for the broken arm. He'd heard her tell the girls that a woman must learn to tend her own aches and sicknesses and those of her family. Doctors were scarce in newly settled parts of the country like central Indiana. For cures folks put a lot of faith in home remedies. "It's

the only way to get through a bad spell," Mother said. Sometimes whole families would be down sick with one thing or another. But the animals still had to be fed and given water, the garden tended, and the crops cared for.

Before Mother finished bandaging Luther's arm, Pap and Ollie were on their way back to the deadening. Though it was a chilly March day, Ollie kept warm cutting and stacking armload after armload of brush and limbs to be burned. What with all this chopping and carrying, his arms ached before the day's work was finished.

It was almost dark when he and Pap went back to the cabin for supper. Just before they left the deadening, Pap set the huge stacks of brush on fire. It wouldn't do to burn them during the day, while he and Ollie were there. The smoke would surely make their eyes sting and their lungs ache.

Against the black night the brush heaps flamed and smoldered. Sometimes they sent sparks shooting up high into the moonless sky with lively snapping and popping noises. From the cabin doorway Ollie called to the others to come look. Louisa and the younger children hurried to see. Out in the deadening the big fires turned the dark night into a blazing, dancing show of golden light.

"Ain't that something?" Ollie cried excitedly.

Even Louisa had to agree with him. "Oh, it is pretty!" But Lucinda said it scared her.

Night after night the fires glowed and flared at the end of each day's work. Then for days afterward all Ollie could smell in the clearing was the trace of the sweet-pungent wood smoke. It clung to the blackened limbs and gray ashes in the deadening, and Ollie wondered if it would ever go away. But day by day the deadening began to look as if it belonged more to the farm than to the forest.

19

FOUR

April

Guess it's time to call in our kinfolk and neighbors for a log-rolling," Pap told his family. "Best way I know of to clear a field in a hurry." It was early April, and Pap had felled the last tree in the deadening. The chopped-down trees, with their limbs trimmed off, had to be rolled together into piles of logs before they could be burned.

Settlers on new land had a way of helping one another, Ollie knew. It was the custom for neighbors and kinfolk for miles around to lend a hand clearing land, or building a cabin, or sharing food, or swapping seeds for crops, or offering home remedies for sicknesses.

Louisa thought a logrolling was a good excuse for folks to get together for a lot of fun and jollification. But it also meant a lot of work for her and Mother and the other women. The children would have to be kept out of mischief, and the men would expect a hearty meal with plenty of food. To Ollie logrollings and cabin raisings were the main social events of the year. They were more fun than they were work. There would be good things to eat and merrymaking, showing off by the boys, and bragging and storytelling by the men.

Pap sent Ollie off on horseback to spread the word. "The folks will be welcome two days from today," Pap stated. He invited all the aunts and uncles and the closest neighbors. He was careful not to invite too many to help, because for every man who came, Pap would have to work one day for them in return. It was the custom.

When the day of the logrolling arrived, it was warm and sunny. "Just right for a gathering," Mother remarked.

The clearing echoed with the early-morning cooing of pigeons and the chirping chatter of robins and tiny finches. Where the land had not been plowed, there were patches of small blue, white, and purple flowers. The young leaves of the trees that edged the clearing were the fresh pale green of spring. And the woods had a sweet, damp smell that Ollie loved.

Soon kinfolk and neighbors, men and boys, women and children began to arrive. There were Mother's brother Ben; Pap's brothers Tom, Jerry, and Milt and their wives; and neighbors— about forty altogether. A few old folks, like Grandma and Grandpa Johnson, showed up, too, just to watch and eat and sit a spell.

"There aren't many old folks in the neighborhood," Mother noted to Pap. Folks knew that a settler's life was hard on a body. The women especially wore out fast—faster than the men.

The women gathered near the cabin to gossip and share the news—the "I heards." The children were quick to disappear off in the direction of the barn, where the grown-ups couldn't see or hear them. There they could run and hide, sing and shout, and be free, with Champ to keep them company.

Ollie stayed near the deadening, where the men were working. Soon it was filled with shouts and loud laughter. There were two squads of men with handspikes, with six men in each. Each man had brought a homemade handspike with him. The spikes were used for both carrying and rolling the logs. One spike could be made from a sapling—a young tree—by trimming all the branches off of it. The finished spike was about three inches thick and six feet long and tapered a little at the ends.

One squad had named Pap captain. Uncle Ben was named captain of the other. "I hope you've got as good a spike as mine, John," Uncle Ben bragged to Pap in a good-natured tone.

Pap nodded at Ben, then at Ollie. Ollie knew the men were bound to stir up excitement, for the settlers loved contests.

The men set to work right away. Uncle Milt, the tail on his old coonskin cap bobbing from side to side, drove the ox team. The oxen and the men working with Uncle Milt moved the logs that were too heavy for the handspike teams to lift. These heavy logs were rolled together to start the heaps, or log piles. There was one heap started for each squad.

Ollie's job was to bring water to the men when they got thirsty. Lifting the logs with the handspikes became a test of strength. In between trips to the well Ollie watched Pap and his men work. When the squad reached the heap, the men on the inside, nearest the pile, put their ends of the spikes down and stepped out of the way. Then the men on the outside lifted their ends of the spikes. A good squad like Pap's could roll a log right down the spikes and onto the heap exactly where they wanted it to go. Sometimes, just to show off, one man would try to lift a log on the handspike by himself. Skill and good common sense were needed to build a pile that would burn down all the way.

The men had been working only a short time when Uncle

Ben called out a challenge to Pap. "If you're able, John, I'll take
you on. My boys can outroll yours any day."

"We'll just see about that, Ben," Pap answered with a smile.
Pap signaled to his men, and right then and there the race was
on. Each squad tried to outdo the other, carrying the logs and
rolling them onto the heaps as fast as they could.

Ollie ran from one heap to the other. He counted the logs
Uncle Ben's squad piled up, then hurried back to Pap's squad to
cheer them on. The higher the heaps rose, the more shouting and
noise there was.

Finally one whole section of the deadening was cleared of
logs and limbs. Pap and Ben told their men to stop. Then Pap
walked over to look at Ben's heap while Ben took a look at Pap's.
Ollie followed along close behind Pap.

"What do you think, Ollie?" Pap asked with a smile.
"Which is the biggest?"

"Speak up, Ollie." Ben winked at his nephew.

To Ollie's way of thinking Pap was the best captain and best handspike man there was. No one hereabouts could beat him, Ollie was sure. But he had to admit, after he looked at each heap, that they seemed almost the same size.

"They look . . . the same, I reckon," Ollie admitted slowly. "But I'd guess the logs in Pap's heap are heavier!" he added quickly.

Uncle Ben threw his head back and started to laugh. Pap and the others laughed too. Then Pap gave Ollie a friendly thump on the back and sent him off to fetch another bucket of drinking water, and the men started working again.

For Mother the dinner was the main feature of the day. Each woman brought a basket filled with something she had made from her favorite recipe.

"Your persimmon pudding looks mighty good, Sarah," said Aunt Polly as she lifted an apple pie from her basket and set it alongside the pudding.

"It did turn out well, Polly," Mother answered. She didn't believe in false modesty. She was known to be one of the best cooks in the neighborhood. But she was careful not to give out the secrets of her recipes. She intended to keep her high standing as a cook.

It seemed to Ollie that the women were as busy trying to outdo one another as the men were. Instead of handspikes, their tools were the bake oven, kettles, and fry pans called three-legged spiders. There was the meat to watch as it roasted over the fire, the johnnycakes to be turned, and the potatoes pinched to see if they were fully cooked.

With the women and girls hurrying back and forth, in and out of the cabin, there was a lot of liveliness to getting dinner ready. By early afternoon the food was spread out for the tak-ing—pork roast, rabbit, venison, corn bread with pumpkin

25

molasses, johnnycakes, baked potatoes, carrots, squash, and, for dessert, persimmon pudding, apple and pumpkin pies, and crab apples preserved in maple sugar.

"This is a spread fit for President Andy Jackson himself!" Pap remarked in a well-satisfied way as he and the other men sat down to eat.

No one disagreed with him.

26

FIVE

May

"Chores are done, Pap," Ollie called as he pushed open the cabin door. The May sunshine brightened the dark inside of the cabin. "Can we leave for Sam Collins's cabin raising now?"

"Set yourself down and eat your cornmeal mush first, Ollie," Pap ordered. "Can't do a man's work unless you eat a man's breakfast."

Mother was busy baking a pie to take to the raising. "I'll bring my pie and the young ones along to the Collinses' later, John," she said.

Pap nodded in answer.

Ollie sat down and ate, but it was hard to hold in the excitement he was feeling. Pap had promised that he could go with him to help raise, or build, the Collinses' log cabin today. This would be Ollie's first chance to work with the older boys and men. A good crew could raise a cabin, log by log, in one day, Pap claimed.

Sam Collins had bought land about a mile to the north of John Johnson's place. Uncle Milt and Sam were the Johnsons' nearest neighbors.

As Ollie and Pap made their way through the woods, Pap told Ollie about the early days in Indiana. "When I brought you and your sister Louisa and your mother up here in 1822, ten years ago," Pap began, "Indianapolis was just one year old—same as you were."

Pap went on to tell Ollie about first coming north in 1821, as soon as the land was opened for settlement. James Monroe was president at the time. The Indians had sold their land in Indiana to the government. Then the government sold it to settlers like Pap. He, his brothers, and Ollie's grandparents came up to the new land from southern Indiana, near the Ohio border. But they did not bring their families right away. First they cleared some land, planted corn, and built a cabin. Sam Collins would do the same.

Pap told Ollie how he built their cabin of logs that were round, just as they had grown, with the bark still on and only their branches trimmed off. "Nowadays," Pap went on, "a man will make his cabin out of hewn logs—logs made flat on two or four sides. That's what I'll do when I add that room onto our cabin soon.

"Sam's lucky," Pap went on. "He's got a good stand of yellow poplars on his place." This clean-smelling wood, Pap explained, was easy to hew with the short-handled broadax. When the wood was green it cut like butter. And yellow poplar logs didn't get all filled with insect pests that liked to live in cracks and under bark.

"They make a fancier-looking cabin," Ollie said, agreeing, "and that's a fact."

When Ollie and Pap reached Sam's, they found about a dozen men and older boys. Each man had brought a tool with him. Uncle Milt had brought his team of oxen to help pull the heavy logs into place. A few men brought long-handled felling axes. These were used to fell the trees. Other men, like Pap, had broadaxes. Their short handles and broad blades made them handy to use for shaping logs or cutting notches in them. One man had an adz. It had a long handle, like a felling ax, and its curved blade was set at right angles to the handle. It reminded Ollie of a short hoe, except the adz was used to smooth the wood.

Soon Ollie and the men were hard at work. Some men felled trees, others hewed logs, and others trimmed branches. The ox team was used to drag four big rocks to the cabin site, the place where the cabin would be raised. There was one rock for each corner of the cabin, which Sam had located near his newly dug well. While the ox team worked, Pap and Sam notched the ends of two long logs. With Ollie's help, after the foundation rocks were in place, they laid these logs on top of the rocks. One log was for the front of the cabin, the other for the back.

"It's mighty tricky getting the floor level and the cabin square," Pap pointed out to Ollie. "It ain't as easy to do as it might look."

Soon Pap and Sam were joined by two more axmen. Now there was one man at each corner of the cabin. Their job was to notch the logs before they were put in place.

Ollie watched as Pap cut the top of the log already in place. "This here's cut so the notch in the next log will sit right snug on top of it," Pap explained. "There's all ways of notching."

29

Ollie could see this made the logs fit snugly, one on top of the other. He helped move the logs into place. First they placed the logs that made the long sides of the cabin, then the short logs at the ends of the cabin.

After the cabin was raised about five logs high, holes were cut for the door, windows, and fireplace. "It's easier and quicker to make the openings this way than to cut the logs before they are put in place," Pap said.

The hole for the fireplace was six feet wide and five feet high. As soon as he could spare the time, Sam would make the fireplace hearth of packed clay and build the chimney. The sides and back of the fireplace would be made from "mud cats." These were a mixture of dried grass and clay. They were shaped by hand into flat blocks about six inches square. Rocks could not be used close to the fire, because the heat would make them crack and split. Pap claimed he once saw one fly apart, with a great bang. Luckily no one had been near enough to get hurt.

By midafternoon the cabin walls were raised eight logs high. The womenfolk had fed everyone well, and this made the heavy work seem lighter. Now the logs for the gables—the topmost

part of the cabin's ends, which came to a point—were laid on top of one another. They would be held in place by the roof.

For the roof, small split logs running the length of the cabin were put in place by two men. The logs ran from one gabled end to the other. These were spaced several feet apart, to hold the roof's shakes. Shakes were like shingles, but much easier to make because they were much larger. Some of the men called them clapboards.

"Ollie, we're ready to lay the shakes and finish off the roof," Pap said. "So you shinny up there and lay them in place the way I tell you to."

Pap split the shakes from short straight-grained oak logs. First he stood an oak log about three feet long on end. Then he took a large wooden maul to hammer the blade of the froe into the log. The froe was a tool with a single blade. Its handle was fastened to the blade at right angles. By hammering with the maul and prying the froe blade back and forth, Pap split off a shake. Then he split another and another from the same short log. Each shake was about three feet long, six inches wide, and about one inch thick.

"Start at the bottom edge of the roof, Ollie." Pap pointed to where he wanted Ollie to start. "You lay a row of shakes there with their long sides almost touching."

Ollie did as Pap told him. Then he laid more shakes over these, to cover the gaps in the bottom layer. The next row was laid so that it overlapped the first row a little, to keep the roof from leaking. Only a few rows were needed on each half of the roof because the shakes were so long. Last Ollie placed long, slim logs, or poles, on top of each row, so they would not blow away in a storm.

Later on, when the weather got warmer, Sam would chink and daub all the cracks between the logs. Chinking was done by pounding short, split pieces of wood between the logs. The pieces were driven in slantwise, one overlapping the other. Then soft clay was daubed, or smoothed, over the top of them. This daubing and chinking was done inside and outside the cabin, to make it snug and tight against the wind and the cold. If a man had a notion to make his cabin fancier than most, he could drag his finger along the soft clay. This would make little ridges in it.

The cabin's rough wood floor was made from puncheons. These were long logs that some of the men split down the middle. Then the flat side, or face, of the puncheon was smoothed with the adz. But no matter how much smoothing was done,

Ollie knew from experience, splinters in bare feet were always plentiful.

Puncheons were also used to make the door, with its wooden hinges. And some were used around the edges of the door and windows to make their frames. The windows were covered with paper, well oiled with bear grease. The grease allowed more light to come through the paper and kept the rain and snow from softening it. The small windows let in only a little bit of light. So summer and winter a cabin didn't have any other light at night except for firelight and sometimes candlelight.

A leather thong was threaded through a hole in the door, about halfway up. Ollie's last job was to fasten this string to the latch, which was a wooden bar inside that held the door shut. When the latchstring was outside, it was a sign of welcome.

"I'm sure tired," Ollie admitted when the work was finished. The cabin had been put up in a day, just like Pap said. And it had not cost a penny to build.

"Not a nail was used in the building," Sam bragged. Nails cost money.

Maybe to some it didn't look very fancy, Ollie thought. Yet he was certain it would make a snug, comfortable cabin, almost as good as his home in the woods.

June–July

The plow blade snagged, then jumped out of the ground. With a snap a tree root popped out of the loosened soil. It nearly jerked the plow handle out of Pap's strong grip.

"A first plowing is enough to spoil the good nature of a preacher!" Pap grumbled. This kind of plow was called a jumping shovel plow, which seemed just the right name to Pap.

Only a week had passed since the cabin raising. Now Pap was getting the deadening he and Ollie had worked on this spring ready for a first planting.

Buck and Bright scarcely seemed to notice the jolting and jerking of the plow. The oxen just batted their eyes and kept on

going at a slow, steady pace. They didn't seem to mind the heavy work or Champ running in and out between their legs. They weren't so fretful as horses, Ollie knew. No lines were needed to drive them. When Pap wanted them to turn right, he hollered "Gee!" And when he wanted them to turn left, he hollered "Haw!"

Ollie went ahead of Pap and the plow, and picked the field clean of blackened log chunks and limbs. This was what was left of the burned log heaps after the logrolling. He threw them onto the brush piled around the edges of the field. The piles made a rough fence to keep out the deer, the cows, and the wild hogs. Later on, when Pap had time, he would move the nearest rail fence so it would protect the new field too. Since the rails weren't pegged or nailed together, they could be taken apart and stacked around the new field. This was one of the handy features of a worm fence. It could easily be moved.

Ollie straightened up to rest for a minute. The field didn't look like much to him. It was dotted with tree stumps, ash heaps, and charred, blackened wood. Though the trees were gone, their roots—which folks called grubs—still lay hidden in the soil.

When Pap finished plowing, the field looked like a scratched-over mess. But after he broke up the clods of soil left by the plow, he planted corn in between the tree stumps.

In a few weeks little sprigs of young corn plants had sprouted all over the field. And by late June the cornstalks had grown taller, and the tree stumps were hidden from sight.

Early one morning in July, Pap announced: "Ollie, I figure you and I should go to town today."

"Gee, Pap!" Ollie was excited. A trip down to Indianapolis didn't come his way very often. And Pap only went every now and then, to buy shoe leather or something needed on the farm.

35

Sometimes Mother went along. "What are you going to get this time, Pap?" he asked.

"Nothing," Pap answered. "I heard the Fourth of July celebration today is going to be the biggest yet. When your brothers get big enough to do the work you do, they'll be welcome to come too."

"Aw, Pap!" Luther complained. Ollie could tell Luther wanted to go pretty bad.

Mother refused to go to town for the holiday. She said it was no place for a woman, what with all those men whooping and hollering and raising a rumpus. Pap said Mother was thinking of the old days, back in the twenties. Nowadays it was different, with the churches and Sabbath Schools taking part in the celebration. Louisa wanted to go, too, but Mother said no, and that was that. Besides, Pap said they were going on foot; Louisa would likely get too tired by the end of the day. So off Pap and Ollie went by themselves.

Indianapolis was the capital of the state, but folks just passing through didn't pay it much mind. They called it only a sprawling frontier settlement. Its main street, Washington Street, ran east–west and was one of the few roadways that was free of tree stumps. The roads leading into town were nothing fancy. Most were cleared wagon paths that wound around tree stumps, forded streams, and followed old Indian trails whenever they could.

There were several churches, cabinetmakers' shops, a blacksmith, a few general stores, a handful of law offices, and the Mansion House and Washington Hall taverns, among others. Work had just started on the building of a statehouse, and the townfolk were mighty proud of this. They also boasted about the Steam Mill Company, which had a sawmill, a gristmill, and a carding mill for flax and wool.

In town Ollie and Pap found Washington Street full of traf-
fic—grown-ups walking, children darting in and out around
them, folks arriving on horseback and in wagons. It was about
ten o'clock when Ollie and Pap passed by one of the churches.

"Why are these folks going to church today, Pap?" Ollie
asked. "It ain't Sunday."

"There's going to be a lot of speechmaking, sermonizing,
and hymn singing," Pap answered, "just special for the Fourth."
To others, he explained, the biggest event of the day would be a
dinner for the militia volunteers. Some would be eating at the
Mansion House, and the others at Washington Hall.

"Who are the volunteers? Are they regular soldiers?" Ollie
wanted to know.

"No," Pap said. "They're like us—farmers, shopkeepers, and
the like. Folks up north thought there was going to be a war.
They said a band of Indians attacked some settlers in Illinois. So
folks hereabouts were afraid of being attacked by Indians too.
Three hundred or more volunteers marched up north, toward
Chicago, to join the fight. But by the time they got there, the
fighting was over. It didn't amount to much." Pap added that the
volunteers came from Marion, Johnson, Hendricks, and Boone

counties. Indianapolis was located in the center of Marion County.

All day long Ollie tried to remember the sights and sounds of the Fourth of July to tell his brothers and sisters about. So when he got back to the cabin at the end of the day, Ollie told about how one of the politicians read the Declaration of Independence. "He made it sound mighty impressive, and the crowd clapped and whistled and hollered afterward. That was at the county courthouse. Then some other men made speeches." Some had spoken in favor of President Andrew Jackson. Others had spoken strong words against him and in favor of his political rival, Henry Clay.

The men tried to outdo one another, Ollie explained. Pap

called this kind of speechmaking political debates. Some of the men were trying to win votes—to be elected sheriff of the county. Others who spoke wanted to be elected to the legislature.

Ollie said he didn't understand much of what they were talking about. But he had a good time watching all the goings-on—the sack and foot races, shooting matches, and horseshoe pitching.

There had been a parade of the volunteers, with drummers and fife players. Flags and banners added color to the march, which started at Governor's Circle in the center of town.

"Independence Day," Ollie declared, "is a lot more exciting than Christmas!"

"That's a fact," Pap put in, sleepy-sounding.

SEVEN

August

During the hot, sunny, humid days of August, Ollie sometimes went down to Fall Creek to go fishing. The black suckers, red horse, and walleyed pike, which some folks called salmon, were so plentiful, he seldom came back to the cabin empty-handed.

Pap was mighty set on Ollie's doing the hoeing, to cultivate the crops. Neither weeds nor grass had grown in the forest because of the heavy shade. But loosening up the soil and chopping out the grubs once the land was cleared was an endless job, Ollie felt. So he liked to slip away from work when he felt he had done enough for one day. Sometimes he let Luther take a turn with the hoe when Pap wasn't around. Then he promised to let Luther go fishing with him.

There were mostly fields of corn to hoe. But there were also
fields of oats, barley, potatoes, beans, and turnips. And there was
always some popcorn that Pap grew for the children. There was
flax, too, so Mother could spin thread to make linen. A neighbor
who had a large loom did the weaving. Then with Louisa's help
Mother sewed linen clothes for the whole family.

Every once in a while Pap would get a woolen coat for himself or Mother or one of the children. These were handed down
until they were worn thin. A few men, like Uncle Milt, hung
onto the old ways, and wore buckskin britches and fringed hunting shirts. Summer and winter he wore his coonskin cap.

Pap liked to recall the time in 1824 when his corn crop was
so small, he had to sell his wedding coat. After he sold the coat
in Indianapolis, he traveled all the way up to Conner's Mill to
buy corn. It was a long trip, eighteen miles north. He bought
enough corn from William Conner to last his family through the
winter.

"It took all of the fifteen dollars I got from the coat to pay
for the shelled corn," Pap added. "Then each time I needed some
of the corn ground into cornmeal, I had to make the long trip
again. It was one of the few mills around in those days." Pap
loved to tell this story to the children. "Makes them appreciate
how easy they have it now," Pap said to Mother.

Pap didn't believe in growing much wheat. "Wheat is enough to make a man choke," he fussed to Mother. "Corn bread three times a day is good enough for me."

Just a few steps from the cabin door, and tightly fenced to keep the animals out, was Mother's garden. There were neat rows of string beans, cabbages, carrots, peppers, onions, peas, and a few cucumbers and tomatoes. In one corner of the garden were herbs—sage, thyme, mustard, and tansy. Some Mother used for flavoring in her cooking. Some she used when the children had a sick spell. Like other pioneer women, she planted this little garden and cared for it herself so her family would have all it needed.

When the tomatoes were red-ripe, she picked them and set them on the fireplace mantel for decoration. Folks said they were poisonous to eat, but they did a lot to make the cabin cheerful-looking. A bowl of them sitting on the mantel or table made a pretty sight.

The last of the tomatoes had just begun to turn from pale red to red-ripe when Sam Collins came by early one morning. He asked Pap to go hunting. His son Abner, who was Ollie's age, came along with him to visit.

Pap always found plenty of game to hunt, for the woods were filled with animals of all kinds. Raccoons, rabbits, and gray squirrels were the easiest to come by. In the fall, when Pap liked to hunt best, there were grouse and turkey and deer. Mostly bears were hunted because they were a threat to farmers' livestock. It was best to hunt the large animals in the late fall or winter, Pap said. The meat would keep fresh in the cold weather. But it would spoil fast if the weather was mild or warm.

Before the men left, Sam said he would like to see Pap's new calf down in the barn. As they leaned their rifles against the side of the cabin, Pap said, "You boys are free to do what you want. No more hoeing for today, Ollie."

As soon as the boys were alone, Abner ran his fingers along the shiny barrel of his father's long rifle. "Let's take the guns and go to the deadening over there," Abner said. "Maybe we can find something to shoot at. My pap won't mind."

Ollie had never gone off with Pap's rifle by himself. Yet without stopping to ask Pap, he took the rifle and followed Abner out to the deadening. He took along Pap's shot pouch and powder horn for loading the rifle.

Within a few minutes the boys sighted a woodpecker not far up on a tree trunk.

"That's a good mark!" Abner cried. "Go ahead, Ollie. Take a shot."

Ollie quickly loaded his father's rifle—first the powder, then the linen patch and bullet. He packed them down with the ramrod. Then he knelt down behind a stump. Resting the rifle on top of it, he took aim and squeezed the trigger. There was a tiny flash as the powder exploded, then a puff of smoke that stung his eyes. He blinked and looked to see if he had hit his mark.

At the foot of the tree lay the dead bird. The shot had hit it in the head.

He was so proud that he had hit the mark, he ran straight off to the barn to show Pap.

Pap looked at the bird, then at Ollie.

Ollie began to feel a little uneasy. Then he remembered he hadn't asked Pap's permission to use the rifle. And Ollie knew Pap was mighty fond of it. He had even given it a name—Long Barrel.

But all Pap said was "Did you aim at the head, Ollie?"

"No, Pap," Ollie answered. "I aimed at the body."

"You did right well to hit the bird. But if you aimed at the body, you should have hit the body."

No more was said. But after this Ollie remembered to ask Pap's permission to take Long Barrel.

September

The hot days of August slipped by until it was almost September. Mother made good use of the oven Pap had built for her outside. It was a lot cooler to cook outside than inside the stuffy, dark little cabin.

With Louisa's help she tended her small vegetable garden. Caring for the garden and milking the cow was woman's work, Pap claimed. Mother agreed, but she said talking to a cow didn't make up for human conversation.

When the summer sun dried the tender young plants, Louisa carried buckets of water from the well to give their thirsty roots a drink. Lucinda toddled along behind, trying to help her older sister. "You keep an eye on her, Louisa, and on Volney and Newton too," Mother ordered. "I have to tend to Baby Elizabeth now."

"Yes, Mother," Louisa would promise, though Ollie knew she wished she could go off and have fun, like he and Luther did when they went fishing.

On one trip to the well she found a toad in the water when she lifted the filled bucket.

"You put that toad down there, Ollie Johnson," she declared, "just to give me a scare!" But Ollie pretended he knew nothing about it.

In September, with the help of the younger children, Mother made soap and dipped candles. The children didn't see the need for soap. But the candles would give light on the long winter's evenings while Mother spun, and Ollie and Louisa did their schoolwork, and Pap read or just sat and chewed and stared into the fire. He wasn't much for conversation, Mother complained. Pap was luckier than many of the older settlers, for he knew how to read. This was one of his main pleasures when he

had the time. His copy of an old history of the world was almost worn through on some pages from being read and reread.

Soon it would be time to harvest the last of the vegetables ripening in Mother's garden. A few would be allowed to grow until they went to seed. Then Mother would gather these seeds and save them for next year's planting. Some she would swap with the other wives in the neighborhood. "It's mostly just an excuse for the womenfolk to get together and gossip," Pap said.

Whatever the reason, Mother looked forward to the swapping and socializing. In the winter she stored the seeds in long-handled gourds she had picked and dried in the fall. During the summer the orange-yellow-green gourds grew outside the cabin, where they made a cheerful and welcoming sight.

Mother liked to pretty up the place, Ollie noticed. Last year she had planted some hollyhocks and marigolds from seeds a neighbor gave her. The reds and pinks and yellows made the little cabin clearing a spot of beauty, Louisa claimed.

Mother was partial to flowers, that was plain. She said she counted them among her blessings. Another blessing, she said, was that no one in the family had got the chills and shakes bad this year. Folks called it the ague. She had heard that, down in the village, almost everyone had had it. Indianapolis, Pap pointed out, was on low, damp land. He didn't think it a very healthy place. It had a lot of swampy patches of land and mosquitoes even thicker than in his woods. Sooner or later everyone came down with the fever. There was no escaping it.

Yet the news Uncle Tom brought from Indianapolis the first week in September wasn't about the ague. He seemed pretty stirred up by it, whatever it was. Ollie drew close to Pap, curious to hear what Uncle Tom had to say.

"Indianapolis is a full-fledged town now, John," Uncle Tom announced proudly. "The citizens had a meeting last night and put together a town government for themselves. Now maybe folks from other parts will sit up and take notice. This ain't the backwoods no more."

"I'll be!" cried Pap. "Ain't that something?"

Ollie didn't see what all the fuss was about. But he tried to look interested, just like Pap.

There was talk, too, Uncle Tom added, of Indiana someday having a lot of canals, fancy gravel-covered roads through the forest—like the east–west National Road that was being built right through the center of the state—and railroads that would connect one town with another.

"Pshaw!" Mother put in. "Just a lot of menfolk's wild talk."

Uncle Tom paid no attention to the interruption. "Indianapolis might be a real important place someday—maybe even a big city, like Philadelphia or St. Louis. It's grown a mighty lot since the state government moved up here from Corydon back in 1825."

Pap said he liked the idea of a town—maybe even a city someday—nearby. After he got more land cleared, he could sell his extra crops to the townfolk for cash. Right now about all he could manage to grow was enough to feed his own family. If there was any extra corn, he traded it in town for what he needed—like shoe leather or a wool coat.

A few days after Uncle Tom's visit, Pap thought it would be a good time to go into town to get the shoe leather he needed this year. He wanted to hear more news about the town. But Mother got after him about making new benches to take the place of the two old rickety ones the children used. "They're just all worn out, John," she pointed out.

So the next morning Pap went down to the creek bottom. There tall white-trunk sycamores lined the banks of the river, standing taller and larger than the red and black haws, wild plums, buckeyes, and pawpaws. The sycamores were only good

48

for their looks, Pap claimed. For the benches he picked out the best-looking blue ash he could find and cut it down. Then he split off two rough boards, long enough for the benches, from the trimmed trunk. Next he smoothed the rough boards and pegged in four sturdy legs on each board. When they were finished, Ollie could see that Pap was proud of his work.

"They look real nice and strong, John," Mother said, admiring the benches. "Someday, when you have the tools and the time, I'd like a four-poster bed. Brother-in-law Tom just made one from some extra black-walnut fence rails, and I thought it looked pretty. And maybe then we can have a mattress filled with feathers instead of hay and corn husks."

Pap didn't say anything. He only nodded.

"But for now," Mother decided, "I'm just pleased to have the new benches."

Sitting alongside the two chairs by the fireplace, the new benches looked mighty handsome.

49

NINE

October

Everyone in the family helped gather and put food by for the winter. Louisa and Lucinda helped Mother hang string beans, red peppers, and strips of pumpkin inside the cabin to dry. And when it came time to go nutting in October, all the Johnsons went into the forest to gather nuts. Mother and Louisa took turns carrying Baby Elizabeth, and Pap carried Newton on his shoulders. Champ tagged along, his tail always wagging, eager to not be left behind.

"Will we see any bears?" Volney asked.

Lucinda squealed with fright.

"Not likely," said Pap, "though your Uncle Milt says he's heard of one in the neighborhood lately."

"Humph!" Mother shook her head. "Milt is mighty good at collecting stories."

The bear was soon forgotten as Ollie, Luther, and Volney made a game of finding the nuts. Mother and Pap and the other children joined in the fun. Pap said if they were lucky, they would get their share of nuts before the raccoons and squirrels picked the forest floor clean.

Pap recalled the year the squirrels came out of the woods "like a gray furry flood." They chewed and ate their way through the whole countryside, he explained, leaving little for the pioneer farmers to harvest. "The fields were stripped almost bare. Never saw the likes of it before," Pap declared. "And I surely hope I never see the likes of it again!"

By the end of the afternoon the children were tired. But the family had gathered a good supply of nuts for the winter.

That night after dark, Ollie was on his way from the barn back to the cabin. Suddenly he heard cornstalks snapping and crackling in the field nearby.

"What's that?" Ollie wondered, alarmed. "All the animals are penned up. Sounds like something mighty big. Maybe it's the bear!"

He ran to the cabin as fast as he could and told Pap what he had heard.

Pap didn't pay much mind to Ollie's fears.

51

"Maybe some wild hogs broke through the fence or brush pile and got into the field. We'll take a look first thing in the morning." So early the next morning Pap and Ollie went out into the cornfield.

"Look, Pap!" Ollie cried. "The fence is all right. There ain't a break in it."

Pap nodded. "You're right, Ollie." Then Pap took a close look at the broken cornstalks. They weren't snapped off in a line or path, but in patches here and there. Some of them were just mashed down. There were still some pumpkins in the field, and bites were taken out of a few of them.

"It was a bear that did this," Pap said. "Those patches of mashed cornstalks were where the bear sat down and reached out to pull the stalks to him. He was looking for ears we missed."

"Gee, Pap!" Ollie said, amazed.

Pap knew a bear was a great danger to livestock, his own and his neighbors'. One bear could do a lot of damage. So right away he sent Ollie off to get Uncle Milt to help him chase the bear. "We'll have to hurry," he said.

As soon as Ollie returned with Uncle Milt, Pap told Ollie and the children to stay near the cabin with Mother until he got back. Then he and Uncle Milt took Champ down to the cornfield. Ollie knew the dog could lead them to the bear.

Champ snorted and sniffed as he trotted back and forth and circled around. With his nose to the ground he soon picked up the bear's trail and ran off after it. The men hurried close behind the dog. Every now and then Champ would give a bark as he followed the bear deeper and deeper into the woods.

The sounds of Champ's barks got fainter and fainter. Then they died out altogether. But Ollie, along with Luther, didn't want to miss anything. So they leaned against the fence in front of the cabin, listening for sounds of the chase. They watched for a long time. Ollie was beginning to think that waiting there was a waste of time. Then suddenly he thought he heard Champ's bark again.

"Sure enough, Luther!" he called out. "I do hear old Champ's bark, and he's headed this way."

Mother and the other children hurried out of the cabin to join the boys. Mother put her hands to her eyes and looked out across the fields. At first she didn't see anything.

Then Luther shouted, "There he goes!" He pointed off to the left to a newly cleared patch of land.

There the bear was, loping along, throwing his front feet first to one side, then to the other. Champ, his tongue lolling out of one side of his mouth, was right behind the bear.

"That bear looks a mite tired," Mother cried.

Ollie had never seen her act so excited before. She stretched up on her toes, cupped her hands around her mouth, and shouted to Champ as loud as she could, "Whoop-ee-ee!"

53

With that Champ darted forward and caught the upper part of the bear's right hind leg in his teeth. Together bear and dog tumbled down in a wriggling heap. Then Champ scrambled to his feet and jumped clear. He turned to charge at the bear again. But by now it, too, was on its feet. It took off toward the woods as fast as it could, with Champ close at its heels.

Pap and Uncle Milt trailed along behind. They acted as if they were out of breath and tired. But they kept on going as fast as they could, trying to catch up.

"Champ will have that old bear up a tree soon," Mother said with a satisfied nod of her head. "Then the men will have a good mark."

It wasn't long after this that Ollie and the others heard the sharp cracks of two rifle shots deep in the woods. When Ollie heard the shots, he knew the hunt was over. Mother had been right—Champ had treed the bear.

The next day the neighbors got a share of bear meat. The meat was nothing fancy to eat, folks said. But the story that Uncle Milt told about the chase was.

....

November—December

A few days after the bear hunt Pap went to town to buy shoe leather. That evening, when the chores were done, he started making the family's shoes.

Beginning in the late spring, all through the summer, and well into the fall everybody went barefoot most of the time. Tough feet, Pap claimed, were a real blessing in a big family. They saved a lot of shoe leather.

By the end of October he had finished his shoes and Mother's as well. Then he started on Louisa's and Lucinda's. Ollie looked forward to having his new shoes to wear to school, but he and his brothers always had to wait till last. Pap didn't work on them every night, but by the middle of November the girls' shoes were done.

Mother fussed at Pap because he was so slow this year. "Sitting by the fire of an evening just thinking and reading ain't going to get shoes made for the boys, John," she told him.

Pap said sometimes he had more important things to do of an evening. "Besides," he added, "it makes a boy healthy to go barefoot when the ground is frosty."

But after this Pap worked some on the shoes almost every night.

Ollie, being the oldest boy, was always the last one to get

his. Well into December he was still going barefoot to school. Sometimes the ground was so cold, his feet ached. As the weather got colder he took to heating a short board in the fireplace before setting out for school. He let it warm in the coals until it began to send up curls of smoke.

When he left the cabin, he stuck the hot board under his arm and ran over the biting frost until his feet began to ache with the cold. Then he stopped, dropped the board, and stood on it. After his feet warmed up a bit, he grabbed the board and ran until his feet got cold again. By the time he got to school, the board was chilled, but his feet weren't numb, and he felt he didn't have anything to complain about.

This year Ollie had plenty of opportunity to toughen his feet. It was close to Christmas before Pap started making Ollie's shoes. Luther had had his for over a week now, and Ollie wished he had his too. Almost all the other boys at school were wearing shoes by now, and he felt left out.

Like most settlers, the Johnsons never made much of Christmas Day. None of the children expected presents; it wasn't the settlers' way. And since Christmas came on a weekday this year,

there would be school as usual. Ollie had little hope he would
have his shoes in time for Christmas.

They sat, still unfinished, by the fireplace on Christmas Eve.
Ollie glanced at them as he left the cabin to do his chores. "No
use wishing anymore," he said to himself, disappointed.

Down at the barn he took his time. The air, though cold,
was crisp and smelled fresh and clean. Sometimes, Ollie thought,
the cabin got a mite smoky because of the fireplace. Also Christmas Eve seemed a good time to give the animals a little extra
attention, especially Buck and Bright and Champ. He wouldn't
let the family know, though, for they would think he was too
softhearted.

It was over an hour later before he got back to the cabin.
When he pushed open the door, he saw Pap standing near the
fireplace, his hands behind his back.

Pap looked angry.

"I've been waiting for you, Ollie," Pap said, not smiling.
"You were gone longer than need be, and I've got something else
for you to do."

Louisa giggled. Then Luther. Then Lucinda. The youngest
children stopped what they were doing to see what would happen.

Pap took his hands from behind his back and handed Ollie
his finished shoes. "Time to try these on." Then he smiled.

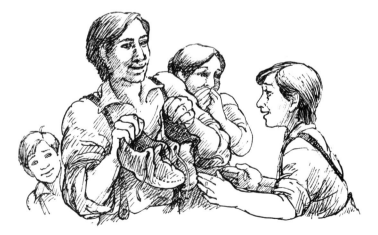

"Gee, Pap!" Ollie cried as he took them. He put them on right away. Then he ran out of the cabin and down to the barn, just to see what they felt like. He forgot about the thin sheet of ice around the water trough. As soon as the slick new leather of his shoes touched the smooth ice, his feet went out from under him. With a thump he sat down hard.

His sisters and brothers laughed when they found out what had happened.

"It ain't a laughing matter!" Ollie shouted angrily, rubbing his backside.

Going to school the next day was more painful than usual, yet Ollie soon forgot his aches and pains. For Schoolmaster Hawkins gave each of the children a Christmas treat—an apple and a fresh-baked ginger cake. He knew if he did not give them a treat, the boys would play a trick on him. This was the custom.

Then he gave them another surprise. "Now you scholars can play games or draw on your slates or just read if you are of a mind to," he said, with a big smile.

The children were so surprised and pleased, they jumped up from their benches and shouted. The schoolmaster laughed, adding to the noise and merriment.

On the way home from school, Louisa told Ollie that it was a Christmas she was likely to remember for a long time.

"Me too," Ollie said cheerfully, "because I got my new shoes. That's a lot more important than just having fun."

"Ollie Johnson!" Louisa said in a scolding tone. "Good times are more important than anything—like the logrolling and the cabin raising and all of us going nutting last fall."

Ollie thought about what Louisa had said. "Well, I did have a mighty good time at the Fourth of July celebration in town. And it's always fun to go fishing down in Fall Creek on a hot day." And maybe best of all, he thought, was Mother's persimmon pudding at the end of a long ride to the mill.

No matter what the task, Mother and Pap had a way of turning work into play. With seven children there was always a lot of work to be done. For some people, like the townfolk, life in a log cabin in the woods was too hard and too lonely, Ollie had been told. But he never thought about its being hard. He had never known any other way of life. And to him there wasn't a lonely spot in the forest—with the trees and the animals and his brothers and sisters to keep him company.

It made for a mighty satisfying life. He couldn't ask for any better.

In 1830, when Ollie was nine, about 1,100 people lived in the village of Indianapolis. Today over a million people have homes in the Indianapolis–Marion County metropolitan area.

Now where Ollie's cabin once stood are the grounds of the Indiana State Fair. Where the bear in Ollie's story was chased through the cornfields, cars now follow one another in six lanes along a busy city boulevard. Winding alongside the boulevard is Fall Creek, where Ollie and Luther fished.

The Johnsons were among central Indiana's first settlers. Pap came as soon as the territory was opened in 1821. The government offered the unsettled land for sale, and Pap bought an eighty-acre tract. In 1822 he brought his family up, from near the southern Indiana–Ohio border, to their new home in the woods.

For Ollie's parents life was filled mostly with hard physical work. Their daily ways and their log cabin were much like those of other pioneers not only in the heartland of the nation, Indiana, but also in the East and in the South. Mother and Pap were realists. They prided themselves on having a lot of common sense. And it was this common sense—not book learning—that helped them with their problems each day. They expected to earn their way.

They also were experienced pioneers, familiar with the dangers, hardships, and never-ending labor of lives lived in a log cabin. Pap was part woodsman, part hunter, and part farmer. Mother's job was to take care of Pap, manage the household and garden, and have as many babies as she could bear.

There would be hard times, good times, sad times, happy times, both Mother and Pap were certain. Yet like their neighbors they were optimists. They looked forward from one year's harvest of crops to the next. They were sure that the future would be brighter than today, and for them this happened.

When Ollie grew up, he bought his own farm, north and a little west of his father's. He married and had children, then grandchildren. To one of them, Howard Johnson, he told stories about what he remembered of his pioneer boyhood. Howard wrote these stories and memories down.

Then when Howard's grandson was a teenager, he and his grandfather built a log cabin in the woods. It was as much like Ollie's boyhood home as they could make it. This cabin stands today within the City of Indianapolis not far from where the Johnson cabin once stood, over 160 years ago.